WHAT HORSE IS THAT?

Peter Roberts &
Sally Gordon

octopus

First published 1980 by
Octopus Books Limited
59 Grosvenor Stree
London W.

ISBN 0 7064 1178 1

©1980 Octopus Books Limited

Produced by Mandarin Publishers Limited
22a Westlands Road, Quarry Bay, Hong Kong

Printed In Hong Kong

CONTENTS

INTRODUCTION

In asking the question 'What horse is that ?', it would be quite possible to receive several answers, all of which would be perfectly accurate. In many cases, the answer might be the name of the breed, for there are more than 200 breeds of horses alive in the world today. Some of these are indigenous to a particular country or region, having bred there for many centuries unaided and unmolested by man. In such events, the horses or ponies breed repeatedly true to type, faithfully reproducing the characteristics that their fore-fathers displayed before them. Such characteristics are likely to be those that give the animal the greatest chance of survival in its particular habitat, for, as always with animals living in the wild, it is those most suited to the rigours of the environment that survive to perpetuate the race.

Other breeds of horses and ponies have been created by man to fulfil a particular need of the time or to satisfy a whim or mode of fashion. Man discovered his ability to create a new breed when he saw that different types of horse and pony could interbreed and observed that characteristics from the mother and father—the mare and stallion—were apparent in the offspring. He made use of this

knowledge to produce horses whose chief attribute was speed, great tractive power, or outstanding beauty. The more breeds he created, the greater were the possibilities of producing even more breeds to satisfy every possible requirement.

But the answer to 'What horse is that?' might not be a breed at all, for not every horse or pony belongs to a recognized breed. Some may be classified as 'types' rather than breeds, the classification in this instance referring to the 'profession' to which the animal is suited. A horse may be called a hunter, for example, which means that he possesses those qualities that would enable him to carry a rider through a day's sport in the hunting field. These are characteristics of conformation and temperament, which may be found in many different breeds of horse. Horses trained to play polo, too, are called

polo ponies, but all sorts of different breeds go to produce them, or alternatively are used in the game.

Other types of horses are categorized by colour. A 'palomino' horse or pony is one that possesses a coat of a particular golden colour with a white mane and tail, but palominos of widely differing appearance and conformation will be seen.

The answer to the question might be neither a breed or a type for literally millions of horses and ponies are cross-breeds, produced by crossing one breed with another. The results of such crosses are not recognized breeds. These animals, however, are the mainstay of the riding fraternity.

It is all these sorts of horses that concern us in this book—the breeds, the types and the 'family pets' of the horse world, that may be put to work in the service of man in a number of different ways.

STORY OF THE HORSE

The story of the horse began almost 60 million years before the story of man. It stretches back to a date so deep in the past that it holds little significance for most of us, and yet that is where we have to go to find the first 'horse'. In common with most other animals, the horse of today bears very little resemblance to its far-off ancestor, which was similar in size and shape to a dog, and possessed a small head, arched back, long bony tail and multi-toed feet.

It took the horse some 55 million years to evolve from this diminutive creature to the single-hoofed, much-loved animal that is found in every country of the world today. The horse as we know it appeared in the last million years, so in fact it is only in its present form that it has been known to man.

Since they first came into contact, man and horse have done much to shape, influence and assist each other's passage through history. To begin with, man followed the wandering horses, relying on them to some extent for food and also for milk from the nursing mares. But then man learnt to be a herdsman and began to guide his 'flock' of grazing animals to

richer pastures, thereby producing healthier stock. Then he discovered that he could sit on the horse's back and ride him in pursuit of other animals, and he could harness the horse to crude sledges and carts to carry his belongings. From that moment the horse became the servant of man.

The story of each individual horse or pony, such as this frolicking foal, generally begins in the spring of the year, for this is the usual time for birth to occur. This is nature's way of ensuring that the newborn foal has the maximum amount of warm weather in front of it in which to grow and develop before the cold and wet of autumn and winter sets in. Within an hour or so of being born, the ungainly foal will struggle to its feet unaided and begin sucking from the mare. Female foals are called fillies and male foals are colts.

THE AMERICAN QUARTER HORSE

Left: Although horses originated in the United States of America all those millions of years ago, they disappeared completely from that continent during the Pleistocene period (1 million to 8150 BC). They were not to reappear in the land until the Spanish conquistadores rode them across the country in the sixteenth century. Since then, many superb breeds of horse have been developed in the United States, and this—the American Quarter horse—is one of the oldest and most popular.

The type of saddle and the lariat indicate that the horse's prime role is as the mount of the ranch cowboy.

THE BEAUTIFUL ARABIAN

Below left: This magnificent horse is known to have lived in the deserts of Arabia for thousands of years, although its actual origins are lost in the annals of history and clouded by myth and legend. Nowadays, Arabians are bred all over the world and slight variations in appearance will be found among the different strains.

All Arabians possess the characteristics shown here—free, fluid movement, high head carriage, flaring nostrils and long, flowing mane and tail.

AMERICA'S WILD HORSE

Left: Mustangs, here seen grazing on the Kansas prairie, are the only wild horses to be found in the USA. They are the descendents of the domesticated mounts of the conquistadores, or at least of the ones that escaped to the wide open spaces. Mustangs are undistinguished to look at, but the rigours and hardships of their habitat have given them an incredibly tough and wiry constitution.

SPOTTED HORSES

Above: The spotted Appaloosa is also an American breed, although spotted horses have long been known in Europe and Asia. Appaloosas were developed by the Nez Perce Indians who prized the spotted horses they found on the plains and began to breed from them at the beginning of the eighteenth century. Now there are six coat patterns of the Appaloosa.

This one is the Leopard whose base coat colour is white. Its entire body is covered in brown spots.

THE LIVING PREHISTORIC BREED

Above: These somewhat rough-looking sandy coloured horses are the most primitive breed alive today. Some people claim that they are actually one and the same as *Equus Caballus*, the prehistoric horse that appeared on earth about a million years ago. The breed was thought to be extinct for many centuries, when a Russian explorer called Colonel Przewalski found a herd of them during an expedition in the wastelands of Mongolia during the 1880s. Some of these horses still inhabit the area, scratching a meagre existence in the inhospitable, arid land. The future of the breed, however, lies with those kept in captivity in zoos around the world. Przewalski horses are always a sandy colour, known as dun, and they generally have a black mane and tail, and black lower legs and dorsal stripe (a line running from the mane straight down the backbone to the tail).

Although they are always called Przewalski horses, they are actually ponies for they stand no more than about 12 hands high. The definition of a pony is an animal that is 14.2 hands high or smaller. If it is taller than this, it is a horse. A hand is a measurement of 10 cm (4 in). The origin of this term is most probably due to the crude method of actually using a hand to measure the height of a horse.

COLOURED HORSES

Above left: The colour of a horse or pony's coat is one of the most important factors to define when giving a description of the animal. There are many different recognized coat colours, with infinite variations of shade within each category. Some breeds have a tendency for various coat colours to predominate and many breeds exclude 'coloured horses' such as this one from entry in the official stud book. The horse in this picture is called a skewbald—that is, its coat features large irregular patches of white and brown. If, instead of brown, the coloured patches were black, it would be known as piebald. In America where coloured horses have long been popular, there is an association known as the Pinto Horse Association. It was formed specifically for the registration of coloured horses.

THE SMALLEST NATIVE BREED

Left: The diminutive Shetland is the smallest of all British native breeds of pony and yet, at the same time, it is one of the strongest and hardiest. Although it is now bred in domestic situations the world over, it can still also be found living wild in its natural habitat—the bleak, inhospitable islands that lie off northern Scotland and from which it takes its name.

Evidence of the Shetland's existence there has been found dating back to about 500 BC and it would seem that even then, the pony had been domesticated and put to use by man. Shetland ponies are never more than 10.2 hands high (105 cm/42 in—a hand measuring 10 cm/4 in) and they are usually considerably smaller. They have a coarse coat which grows very thick and fluffy in the winter to protect them from the extreme cold. The full, long mane seen in this illustration is another characteristic of the breed.

JUMP!

Strange as it seems in the light of the enormous popularity of jumping on horseback today, it is probable that a little more than 200 years ago, few horsemen (except those in the army) had ever thought of putting their horses at a jump. In fact, horses are not natural jumpers—although all can be taught to jump—and to the great majority of riding people there would have been no need to indulge in such an unnecessarily dangerous pursuit.

In Britain it was mainly the Enclosure Acts of the 18th century that turned horses and horsemen into jumpers, for now suddenly there were obstacles in the way of the line of hounds pursuing the fox when hunting. If the mounted followers were to keep up with the day's sport, they had somehow to overcome the obstacles in their way. From this beginning, competitive jumping later came into its own.

The early showjumping competitions, which began in the late 19th century, were known as leaping contests and were a far cry from the colourful sophisticated spectacles of today. Course building was an unknown skill and as a result, a show-jumping course usually consisted of seven straight-forward fences. Six were put round the outside of a rectangular ring with the seventh in the middle. Competitors rode around the jumps taking as long as they liked, even getting off to adjust a piece of saddlery in the middle of the round if they felt like

EVENTING'S LEADING LADY

Lucinda Prior-Palmer has been able to claim the title 'leading lady event rider' for some time, so consistent have her successes been since she first appeared on the scene. She started on her road to fame as a member of the winning team in the Junior Three Day Event Championship in Germany in 1971 and since then she has never been out of the limelight. Probably her most famous horse is *Be Fair*, with which she came fifth at the Badminton Three Day Event in 1971 when she was only 18 years old. Two years later she came first in this event, a position she held again in 1976 on *Wide Awake* and 1977 on *George*.

In this picture she is seen riding *Village Gossip* as they make a stylish jump over the testing Normandy Bank at the Badminton Three-Day Event in 1978.

it. The judging system was complicated and open to argument so that the competitions often went on far into the evening. They were certainly very different from today's exciting competitions.

Eventing has a longer and rather more distinguished history than showjumping—its upstart cousin. Although its origins can be traced back even further, it mainly belongs to the 16th century era of the great European riding academies. The purpose of the academies was to train army officers and their horses to produce a duo of the highest calibre and ability. Eventing, or combined training as it is also called, proved the ideal training for such an aim as it combines three quite different fields of horsemanship. First there are the disciplined movements of dressage, followed by the courage and skill of riding and jumping a cross-country course at speed and finally the control and timing necessary for showjumping.

Three day event competitions as they are today began at the beginning of this century when they were understandably dominated by the military. Since then they have become increasingly popular with civilian riders, who now take most of the prizes.

The part of the event that always draws the biggest crowds is the cross-country phase. Thirty or so fences are set out over a course that is generally about 8 km (5 miles) long.

THE PENGUIN PIT AT WYLYE

Above left: Mrs Brown and her bay mare, *Tequila*, clear the jump called the Penguin Pit at the Wylye Horse Trials. This three-day event is held each year in the autumn. It has the reputation of having a well-built, but not too difficult cross-country course and consequently it is one that many young riders enter as their first international event. As with all major horse trials, the cross-country course is changed slightly each year, so that horse and rider are faced with a new set of trials and tribulations each time.

Most horse shows and competitions depend on sponsorship of some kind, either to help pay for the organization of the event; the building of the course or to put towards the prize money. At Wylye, individual firms sponsor a jump—that is they put up the money needed to build it. This fence was sponsored by a company called Penguin Swimming Pools, which is how the jump comes to have its name.

THE LONELINESS OF THE EVENTER

Below left: Eventing is by no means just about jumping. In addition to the main events—the dressage, crosscountry jumping and showjumping courses—a competitor has to complete a speed and endurance test staged over a distance of about 24 km (15 miles). This includes a 3 km steeplechase course which does contain several jumps similar to those seen on a steeplechase course. The test is across roads, fields and tracks. The test has to be completed within a prescribed time and a rider gains no extra marks for completing it more quickly. The wise rider tries to make full use of the time allowed, thereby reducing the risk of tiring his mount unnecessarily before the truly demanding cross-country course. This, the pair have to begin just ten minutes after completing the speed and endurance test.

Horses used in eventing are not of one particular breed, although there are a number of definable characteristics to be found in successful eventers. They must be bold and courageous—willing and able to jump formidable fences at speed. They must be agile and versatile, happy to execute disciplined dressage movements one day and pound round a cross-country course the next. They have to be strong, good-natured and calm so that they are not easily upset by the different demands placed upon them. Above all, they have to be completely obedient to the commands of their rider.

THE WATER JUMP

Above: Derek Ricketts and his horse *Nice 'n' Easy* spread themselves out in classic style at the water jump in the British Jumping Derby held each year at Hickstead. As in eventing, no specific breed of horse is *always* to be seen in the showjumping ring. The necessary requisite for a showjumper is that it is a top-class athlete—able and willing to jump huge, brightly-coloured obstacles in cold blood, that is for no better reason than because its rider requires it to do so.

The water jump is particularly testing, for in order to clear the spread the horse has to approach the fence at high speed. He will then have to steady up quickly immediately after the jump in order to take the rest of the course at a controlled pace.

THE DERBY BANK

Above: This is an unusual obstacle for a showjumper to encounter, but all those who have competed in the British Jumping Derby at Hickstead will have done so for it is part of the permanent course at this show ground. The British Showjumping Derby is one of the most important events in the showjumping calendar and has been held annually at Hickstead since 1961. The Hickstead show ground is unique in Britain in that it possesses a permanent showjumping course. It was modelled on similar arenas found in Europe, and indeed the British Jumping Derby itself is modelled on a similar event that used to take place each year in Hamburg. Of course, many of the jumps are not permanent and change with each competition each year, but others like the bank which dominates the arena, are clearly immovable. Horse and rider have to jump onto the bank, take some strides along the top of it, before jumping or sliding down the steep slope seen here. Paddy McMahon, one of Britain's leading figures in the showjumping world, is seen negotiating the bank in classic style. Note how even though the horse is at a severe angle, the rider still leans forward. By leaning backwards, however much safer it might feel, too much weight would be placed on the horse's hindquarters.

INDOOR SHOW JUMPING

Left: The competitive world of show jumping as we know it really began indoors with the first International Horse Show. This was held in the indoor arena at Olympia in London in June 1907, the stadium shown in this picture. The course, and indeed the whole competition, would have been very different then from the present-day sponsored shows, which are now held each year just before Christmas. Nowadays it is the indoor shows that attract the top names in the world of show jumping, for generally they are able to offer much higher sums in prize money than most of the outdoor shows. This is because the firms and companies that sponsor show jumping—such as Radio Rentals who are the sponsors of this show—favour the indoor shows, knowing that the excitement and tension that goes with the jumping of huge fences in such a confined area attracts huge television audiences. Horses that perform well in outdoor arenas do not always do well when brought into the tiny ring with its bright, glaring lights and atmosphere of expectancy and excitement.

THE CONTROVERSIAL FIGURE

Above: Harvey Smith, seen here jumping immaculately on *Lights Out* is the showjumping rider the spectators love to hate! Ever since he first became a leading figure in the sport in the early 1950s, he has aroused continuous interest and controversy with his outspoken views and his sometimes rather unorthodox behaviour and tactics in the ring. Whatever his critics may say, however, Harvey Smith's success cannot be denied, and during the course of his career he has won nearly every major competition in the British showjumping calendar as well as having enjoyed similar success overseas.

Harvey Smith's first horse—in the world of international showjumping that is—on which he jumped with the British team in Dublin in 1958 was called *Farmer's Boy* and cost Harvey just £40. A showjumper of *Farmer's Boy's* calibre would probably cost about a hundred times that figure today.

THE RUSSIANS ARE COMING

Right: All the major countries of the world now participate in international showjumping events and representatives travel far and wide to compete. Here, a Russian horseman makes a rare appearance in this country, and it is obvious that neither horse nor rider are new to the sport. By and large, however, the Russians have not distinguished themselves greatly in the international equestrian showjumping

scene, but have enjoyed considerably more successes in the dressage world.

The Russian riders took the team gold medal for dressage in the 1972 Olympics at Munich as well as the individual silver. In 1970 they won the World Championships in Aachen and in 1974 they came second. They have also figured consistently in the top three in the European Championships since 1965. Perhaps showjumping results of the future will show a similar dominance!

TROUBLE AHEAD!

Above: Look at the pony's hind feet in this picture—disaster must lie ahead, for as it brings down its feet, it must bring the pole with them. Considerable further damage could come about if the pole gets tangled up in the pony's legs.

It would appear that the pony misjudged its stride as it came into the jump and took off too early. It has had to really stretch itself forward in an effort to clear the fence. The other eventuality when a horse or pony misjudges its stride coming into a jump is to take an extra short stride before taking off, so it is then too close to the fence. Instead of having to stretch itself to clear the obstacle, it is then forced to 'cat jump'—that is to lift the forelegs sharply and then to twist the hindquarters over the jump. It can be extremely unseating for the rider, and can be avoided when the rider has more experience.

23

BETWEEN THE SHAFTS

Before modern machines and transport were known, the horse was a common sight everywhere between the shafts of a cart or carriage, a farm implement or wagon. For centuries, horses provided the sole means of transportation on land and in fact they pulled the barges on the rivers and canals too. Without them the farmer could not have reaped his harvest and many other craftsmen and workmen could not have even begun their daily work.

Today the role of 'working' horses lives on although out of necessity the emphasis has both shifted and changed. Less frequently are they seen helping to cultivate the land, although in some parts of the world they are still essential to the smooth running of remote farming communities. Gone are the horsedrawn barges and stage coaches, but new eras bring with them new needs and requirements and the 'coach' horse can be seen in other guises

today. The tourist industry, for example, uses horses trained to operate 'between the shafts' to take tourists round major cities in open carriages, or to pull 'gypsy' caravans round quiet lanes.

On a more practical level, many breweries use heavy horses to pull their loaded drays to make deliveries to pubs close to the breweries. City-based firms and companies use smart horse drawn cabs as part of their promotional campaigns and also to make local deliveries. The rag-and-bone man with his scruffy pony and paint-stripped cart loaded with the most useless-looking junk is still a feature of many places. Police forces the world over have long used horses in their daily work, patrolling the streets or controlling crowds at football matches or protest rallies. They still play a vital role in army regiments in many countries.

In remote areas, horses are still used as pack animals to carry all manner of cargo. And out in the 'Wild West', the ranch cowhands could not go about their daily work among the cattle if it were not for their tough little cow ponies.

THE FARM WORKERS

Previous page: This superb scene of two heavy horses drawing a hand held plough was once a common sight in all rural, farming areas. Now it is rarely seen outside of specially organized ploughing contests which incidentally have been taking place since the early 18th century. The 'gentle giants' seen between the chain shafts of the plough (jobs like ploughing and drilling where the machine is attached to the horse's harness by chains are termed 'working in chains') are Clydesdales.

They come from the county of Lanarkshire in Scotland where they were first produced in the mid 18th century. Native mares were crossed with the very heavy Flemish stallions in order to produce a heavy working horse capable of hauling coal from the Lanarkshire coalfields. From their earliest appearance, they were sought after for farm work.

THE TALLEST HORSE IN THE WORLD

Above: The docile Shire, seen above, has the distinction of being the tallest horse in the world and has been known to exceed 18 hands high.

Aptly named, the horse is found in the central shire counties of England; it is said to descend from the Great Horse of Tudor times—a horse developed specially for the task of carrying the heavily-armoured knights of this period. Since its first appearance, the Shire has been one of the stalwart workers of agriculture, but like other heavy horses, it became largely redundant when mechanization swept through farming operations. A recent revival in interest in all breeds of heavy horse has made the Shire's future look considerably less bleak than it had for some years and now it is finding new employment between the shafts of tradesman's carts such as this one.

THE OLD DAYS REVIVED

Above: A parade of heavy horses reliving their role in agriculture brings a touch of nostalgia to a modern setting. Note the horse brasses in this and the picture opposite (worn down the chest). These have been found on old harnesses dating back a hundred years or more and were said to ward off the 'evil eye'—that is avert any mishap that might befall horse and owner during the course of their daily toil.

LUNCHBREAK FOR THE WORKERS

Left: When horses were the only means of land transport, it was a common sight to see them at rest by the side of the road or on the edge of a field, their noses buried deep in nosebags. These ones are made of leather, although they were more normally constructed of tough sacking or hessian. As can be seen, they have a long strap which is buckled over the horse's head. A small feed inside of mixed corn and chaff (chopped hay) provided a welcome snack for those who had pulled a heavy load all morning and were faced with a similar prospect throughout the afternoon.

THE KING'S TROOP

Both these illustrations portray the officers and horses of the King's Troop, Royal Horse Artillery, pulling the Troop's magnificent gun carriages. The King's Troop was established in 1947 at the command of King George VI who had said he would like a troop of the Royal Horse Artillery to take part once again in the great ceremonies of State after the war. This Troop, he said, should be known as the King's Troop and that name lives on today in spite of the fact that the reigning monarch is a Queen.

The headquarters of the King's Troop is at St John's Wood in London and this is where the horses in active service are kept. Most of the horses are purchased in Ireland when they are between four and five years old. At this stage they are not broken-in—that is they have not been trained to carry a rider or operate in harness. The horses purchased by the troop may be any colour from light bay through to black, and they vary in size from about 15.3 to 16.1 hands high. The differences in height and build are attributable to the different tasks required of the horses. Those at the front of the team of six that pull the gun carriages must be strong and able to exert great tractive power, while those at the back must be smaller and stockier as their job is to act as a brake on the carriage when it is turning or coming to a halt. These horses, known as 'wheelers', exert very little pulling power and yet are of obvious vital importance.

The gun carriages pulled by the horses each weigh 1.5 tonnes and were all used in active service during the First World War. A team of horses together with the gun carriage is 18 m (20 yd) long.

AT WORK IN NORWAY

Above: This little pony waiting patiently while its cart is loaded with grass cut from a roadside orchard is the Fjord pony, the native pony of Norway. It has lived there since the days of the Vikings, and has changed little in appearance over the centuries. Its most outstanding characteristic is its mane, which stands upright like a scrubbing brush and has a central ridge of black hairs, flanked on either side by a line of silver ones. Even in these days of modern machines the Fjord pony is much used in rugged and rural mountain areas.

A TEAM OF PALAMINOS

Right centre: Four extremely handsome and perfectly matched Palaminos are seen here pulling a smart, open carriage through the Swiss countryside. Palamino horses are a *type* of horse rather than a breed, and may be any size or shape as the term refers to the colour only. However, the colour is extremely important and unless a horse or pony conforms to the standard laid down by the various Palamino Societies, it will not be recognized as a true Palamino, and will be ineligible for registration. The colour of the coat should be 'three shades lighter or darker than a newly-minted coin' and the mane and tail should be white.

AT HOME IN THE WELSH HILLS

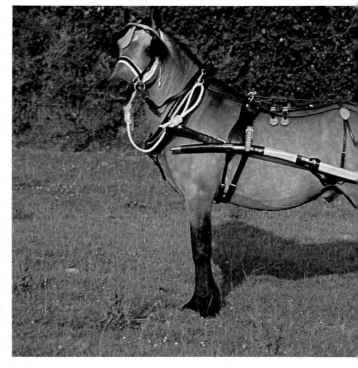

Right: This perky little Welsh Mountain Pony looks to be carrying all the family's livestock in his low two-wheeled cart! The Welsh Stud Book, in which details of the Welsh Mountain Pony are found, has three other sections as well. The Welsh Mountain Pony, section A (like the one pictured here) is for those ponies that do not exceed 12 hands high, section B is for ponies similar in appearance to the Welsh Mountain Pony, but standing up to 13.2 hands high, and sections C and D are for Welsh ponies and horses of rather

stockier appearance. The Welsh Mountain Pony section A formed the foundation stock for all the other sections. The pony is known to have lived wild in the Welsh hills at least since Roman times, a life-style some still enjoy. Far more, however, are now bred in domestic situations as they are widely sought as children's riding ponies and as small harness ponies like this one.

A GYPSY'S LIFE

Above: Brightly painted caravans pulled by scruffy, but well-cared-for horses of humble birth were once a common sight in rural Britain. They were the homes of the gypsies—nomadic people who preferred a life of gentle wandering to the settled 'bricks-and-mortar' existence of most of us. Nowadays there are few gypsies left and those that there are rely on modern caravans and pick-up trucks to convey them from one site to the next. The traditions of gypsy existence live on in the tourist industry and many holiday companies now offer 'gypsy caravan holidays'. Holiday makers are given a crash-course in how to drive and care for the horse after which they are free to wander the country lanes.

HORSE-DRAWN TAXI

Above: A fine example of how the function of the carriage horse has shifted. Where once horses like these would have been a common sight in the streets of most major cities, pulling the carriage of the wealthy, now they are used as an advertising gimmick and tourist attraction. These horses and the carriage, owned and operated by a hotel in the Swiss resort of Zermatt, spend their time conveying guests to and from the railway station or around the town. The carriage, incidentally, is similar to those that would have been used to fulfill this task in Victorian times.

THE GOODS CARRIERS

'Brandy for the Parson
'Baccy for the Clerk
Laces for a lady, letters for a spy
Watch the wall, my darling while
   the Gentlemen go by!"

Right: So runs a poem by Rudyard Kipling describing just some of the booty carried by packhorses like these in the days when smuggling was rife and horses were the only means of carrying the illegal haul inland from the coastal

regions. The task executed by the packhorse is another job for the 'working horse' that is gradually dying out, although in some parts of the world, where roads are little more than narrow mountain tracks quite inaccessible to motor vehicles, these sturdy ponies are still of vital importance in the safe carriage of goods.

SIGHTSEEING BEHIND THE SHAFTS

Above: Another participant in the tourist industry carries a full load of sightseers around the city of Bruges. This four-wheeled open carriage is designed to carry four passengers who sit in pairs facing each other, with the driver sitting in front of them on a raised platform. The pretty blue-roan coloured pony—the term used to describe a coat colour in which the overall even mixture of black and white hairs results in a bluish tinge—is wearing a 'breast harness'. Compare this to the collar harness being worn by the horses in the opposite picture and you will see that it features a broad band of leather across the chest instead of a collar around the neck. The leather blinkers attached to the harness on either side next to the eyes and worn by all harness horses were originally designed to prevent the animal being frightened by the carriage, wagon or machine it was pulling. It confines the vision to the line directly ahead.

THE ENTERTAINERS

Horses must top the bill for four-legged stars in the immensely varied world of entertainment. In circuses, movies, fêtes and carnivals, military displays, ceremonial occasions and rodeos the horse plays an essential part. In most instances their docile and gentle nature, their willingness to learn and desire to please, and their intelligence and receptiveness to training make them superb candidates for such events.

In some aspects of entertainment, horses are trained to the peak of their natural ability whilst in others, special or trick training is required The famous Lipizzaners from the Spanish Riding School of Vienna for example, which entertain audiences all over the world with their magnificent displays of haute école work, only perform movements that are natural to them. An untrained foal might be seen performing similar movements as it leaps and prances around the field in a show of high spirits. The same is generally true of the horses that take part in the

musical rides of a military display. Whilst they are trained to the highest degree in split-second timing, precision and obedience to their rider's demands, they seldom include in their act any unnatural paces or movements.

Circus and movie horses on the other hand are often taught tricks for their performances. A circus horse might be taught to kneel to take its bow at the end of its act, while movie horses are taught to rear up or fall at a cue from their rider.

The magnificent horses that add so much splendour and pageantry to a ceremonial or State occasion know no such tricks, but they have to be endlessly calm, patient and obedient as they pass the cheering, waving crowds, with all their distracting noise.

Horses of quite a different type and temperament are the stars of the exciting rodeos held in the United States of America, Canada and Australia. Now it is the bucking broncos' turn to delight the crowds with their twisting, heaving antics as they attempt to unseat their tenacious riders.

MUSICAL RIDE OF THE CAVALRY

Previous page: For those who live in the centre of London, the mounted officers of the Household Cavalry are a common sight. They may be seen throughout the year at Horse Guards Parade where each day they provide the Queen's Life Guard.

Here, they are seen performing their musical ride, the most famous section of which is the breathtaking Quadrille. This version of the basic musical ride was first performed at the Royal Tournament in 1880. Eight remount riders in stable dress, eight mounted dutymen, eight state trumpeters and two mounted drummers take part in this parade.

REVIEW OF THE HOUSEHOLD CAVALRY

Above: In this picture, the Major General Commanding the Household division and the General Officer-in-Charge of the London district of the Household Cavalry make the annual review of the Mounted Regiment in Hyde Park. The Household Cavalry is formed from two regiments—the Life Guards and the Blues and Royals (Royal Horse Guards and 1st Dragoons). Each regiment supplies one mounted squadron. The two combine to uphold their traditional three hundred-year old role as the Cavalry of the Royal Household in London. They provide a Sovereign's Escort on all State occasions, such as the Trooping of the Colour and the Opening of Parliament.

KING'S TROOP ANNUAL REVIEW

Below: Like the Household Cavalry, the mounted officers of the King's Troop take part in an annual review when horses and men, looking their shining best, walk past their General and Commanding Officer. The annual review is held in Regent's Park in London, which is not far from the Troop's barracks. The King's Troop undertakes a number of ceremonial duties taking part in the Royal Tournament each year and also performing its famous musical ride at a number of agricultural shows and military tatoos. Seventy-six officers and soldiers take part in this and they end by firing the guns mounted on the gun carriages (see page 28).

The Troop also takes part in the official ceremonies held each year in London on Armistice Day and the Lord Mayor's Show. It fires the Royal Salute in Hyde Park on Royal anniversaries, and provides a gun carriage and team of black horses for State and military funerals.

THE RED-COATED MOUNTIES

Left: The Royal Canadian Mounted Police or the 'Mounties' is probably the most famous police force in the world. It was formed in 1873 when it was called the North-West Mounted Police. One of its unenviable tasks then was to police the wild north-west territories, trying to establish law and order among the Indians who had lived there ungoverned for generations. This duty was combined with the general enforcement of law and order, and the Mounties fame for 'getting their man' became legendary. Fifty years after they first began their operation, their duties were extended to cover the whole of Canada, and having already been granted the title of 'Royal' some years earlier, they became The Royal Canadian Mounted Police.

Nowadays the Mounties can add another role to their list of duties—that of ambassadors, in which guise they travel the world to give performances of their famous musical ride, as they are doing here in the grounds of Cardiff Castle. Just when or why the first musical ride of this sort took place is not known definitely but it is thought to have first been performed as a sort of cavalry drill by British regiments. Today many mounted regiments perform variations of the musical ride, that of the Mounties being among the most spectacular of all. Thirty-two men, mounted on the gleaming black horses bred at the Force's headquarters in Fort Walsh, take part and perform a number of complicated, beautifully timed movements and figures at a trot and canter.

HORSES OF THE BIG TOP

Horses are among the most popular entertainers of all at the circus, and circus horses can be divided into three types. There are the high school horses (*above*) which perform with a rider and execute movements akin to those of a high school dressage horse. Then there are the magnificent Liberty horses that perform superbly-timed movements at the command of their trainer who stands in the centre of the ring. Finally there are the Rosinbacks—the bare-back riding horses, upon which the circus artists stand, turn somersaults, build human pyramids and execute other highly skilled, athletic manoeuvres.

The choice of horses for all these acts is extremely important. The high school horses generally perform on their own, and unlike the Liberty horses do not have to be chosen to match companions in height or colour. Big thoroughbreds are favoured for this type of work, because they look more impressive and display their action more spectacularly than the smaller Arabs or Lipizzaners. They are the aristocrats of the circus ring, and although they are harder to train, they can be schooled to a much higher standard than other circus horses. As well as classical dressage, these horses are taught tricks. One of these is being demonstrated in the picture above, as the horse takes a final bow.

Arabs are the usual choice for Liberty horses. They are smaller, shorter-backed and more manoeuvrable. Stallions are preferred to mares as they tend to show themselves better. They have a calmer temperament than thoroughbreds and require less training. Their shorter bodies enable more horses to fit into the ring, which is an advantage.

The Rosinback horse related to the carthorse. It should have a wide, level back, without a pronounced dip, and should be able to canter evenly and rythmically round the ring without breaking or changing its pace. It needs to have an extremely placid temperament and not mind people leaping on and off its back. The name Rosinback comes from the resin that is rubbed into the horses back to help the artists to grip when riding or standing bare-back.

In comparison to other horses who work for their living, the circus horse has an easy life. It has a training session every morning which lasts for about half an hour, when it exercises and rehearses, and it performs for ten to fifteen minutes, twice a day. It is well-fed and well-groomed. Because of their easy life, circus horses often live to a ripe age. Their feet are never shod as they never work on hard ground.

THE FAMOUS WHITE STALLIONS

Above and far left: The white Lipizzaner stallions of the Spanish Riding School of Vienna are world famous for the school has taken its famous displays of haute école to many countries.

The word 'Spanish' refers to their origin. Today they are bred at Piber in Austria and are taken to the school if they are considered suitable. Their exhaustive training is in the art of classical equitation, which includes dressage movements known as the airs, on and above the ground. The horse above is performing the *Levade,* one of the airs on the ground. The horse's hindquarters are deeply bent so that its body is at an angle of 45 degrees to the ground while its forelegs are drawn up beneath it.

HAUTE ÉCOLE

Left: In this unusual picture an officer from the French Cadre Noir puts his horse through its paces in the collecting ring at Wembley, while famous show jumpers are waiting to go into the arena to jump. Like the Spanish Riding School of Vienna, the Cadre Noir is one of the last outposts of classical equitation. Formed in 1814 at Saumur in France as the Royal Cavalry School, its aim today is to train riding instructors who are then able to maintain and perpetuate the art of classical equitation.

HARAS DU PIN

Above: These magnificent Percheron horse with their red-coated coachman and attendants are included in this section because they also give public displays for the public. They are seen here in front of the impressive buildings of the state-owned and run stud, Haras du Pin, in France. This stud was established at Le Pin in 1728. It took 13 years to build the beautiful chateau and superb stone and brick stables, with its horseshoe-shaped Court of Honour. The first stallion was brought there in 1730, since when there have always been stallions of various breeds at the stud, which over the years, has passed from Royal to Imperial, and finally to State ownership. Currently there are between 80 and 100 stallions at Le Pin, ranging from the heavy Percherons pictured here to the French racing Thorough-breds and Trotters.

THE WINDSOR GREYS

Above right: These beautiful grey horses (even horses with seemingly pure white coats are termed greys) are the most famous of all the carriage horses used by the Royal family on State occasions. Windsor Greys drew the Queen's coach and that of George VI on their respective coronations. The Windsor Grey is not a recognized breed of horse, but became so called after a stud was started in Windsor for the Royal carriage horses. George I brought cream horses to the stud from Hanover. The English stud was disbanded during the last war but later grey horses were once again purchased for the Royal carriages.

Through the centuries all manner of colour and type of horse has been used to draw the State coaches on ceremonial occasions, but it is interesting that chestnut horses have rarely, if ever, been used. The coach in this picture is the Irish State coach, which is the one the Queen usually uses for the State opening of Parliament. This is a copy of the original one which was built in 1851, but destroyed by fire in 1911.

THE ROYAL MEWS

Left: The horses and coaches belonging to the Royal household are kept in the Royal Mews, to which this is the entrance. The present building stands in the grounds of Buckingham Palace and was built in 1825 when George IV commissioned John Nash to redesign the royal stables and coach houses.

The word mews is derived from a French word and was originally used to describe the place where the King's falcons were kept during their moulting period. The name came to be associated with horses when the royal stables were burnt down in the early 16th century and Henry VIII, then reigning monarch, had the horses moved to the mews at Charing Cross. Housing for the Royal horses is as palatial as might be expected. Originally the horses were kept in stalls (three-walled compartments within the main building, the open side facing onto a central corridor to allow access for the grooms) but in recent years, some of the stalls have been converted to loose boxes. (A loose box is a completely 'self-contained room', where a horse may be kept without being tied up as it must be in a stall). Usually it is only the carriage horses that are kept in the Royal Mews—the Royal family's riding horses are stabled mainly at Windsor Castle.

Besides the Windsor Greys, popular types of horse to pull the royal coaches are Cleveland Bays—tall, elegant horses that originated in Yorkshire—and distinguished Oldenburg horses from Germany and Irish-bred horses.

INDIANS AT THE CALGARY PARADE

Above: The Calgary Exhibition and Stampede is a unique event. It began in 1912 when a cowpuncher managed to persuade four wealthy cattlemen in southern Alberta to finance a venture he called the Stampede, which was to be the 'Greatest Frontier Days Show or Roundup' ever held in North America. Today it more than lives up to this title and the annual spectacle which goes on for ten days has parades, exhibitions, ceremonies and demonstrations as well as competitions featuring all the traditional rodeo events—plus a few more besides! Established on the exhibition ground is an Indian village in which representatives from four tribes live throughout the show. They take part in the parades, as well as giving displays of handicrafts and performances of traditional Indian dances.

RODEO THRILLS

Centre right and opposite: A cowboy successfully ropes a galloping steer in the steer roping contest at a rodeo. Now he must jump from the saddle, throw the animal to the ground and tie it up as if the steer were being caught for branding. It is a race against time in which a horse plays a vital part. It must know just how to pursue the steer and cut off its path if necessary. When the cowboy has roped the calf, the horse strains back, keeping the rope tight so that the struggling steer can not free himself. Although this is a timed event, a competitor will be awarded penalty points if he handles the steer with undue roughness.

In the picture on the right, a cowboy is demonstrating exceptional prowess with a lariat. All cowboys must be able to handle a lariat with ease and must be able to lasso a careering steer from a galloping horse—a feat which takes hours of patient practice.

Besides calf or steer roping, the classic events of all

rodeos are bareback and saddle bronc riding, steer wrestling and bull-riding. In steer wrestling, the rider chases after a galloping steer, while another rider helps to keep it on a straight line. Drawing level with it, the rider throws himself off his horse onto the steer's horns and wrestles it to the ground. Bull riding is one of the most dangerous of all rodeo events, in which a cowboy tries to stay on the back of a bucking, twisting bull for eight seconds. The danger lies in the fact that unlike a horse, a bull will turn on its rider once it has succeeded in unseating him. Probably the most famous and popular event of all are the bucking bronc riding events in which a rider must stay on the animal's back for eight seconds if riding it bareback and eleven seconds if the animal is wearing a saddle. All sorts of rules attach to this, for it is not just a matter of staying on—the rider has to exercise a number of points of style too. Many people think that the bucking broncs must be badly treated to behave this way, but in fact this is not so. You can not train a horse to buck—he either does or he doesn't, and if he does, it is probably because he enjoys doing so!

'HIGH SCHOOL' IN HUNGARY

Above: Here a gaily dressed rider in Hungary appears to be putting his horse through its paces before performing in front of an admiring crowd. Besides participating in processions, horses are often used in the special shows and performances associated with fêtes.

On some festive occasions, a group of riders perform a musical ride or carousel. Other performances will be of high school equitation, when a highly trained horse is put through the movements of classical equitation. Like the Lipizzaner from the Spanish Riding School of Vienna on page 40, this horse is attempting a *levade*. Compare the two pictures, though, the hind legs of the horse in this illustration are not yet sufficiently bent beneath him nor are the front legs tucked into the chest far enough for a true *levade*.

CARNIVAL TIME

Left: Carnivals and pageants the world over would lose much if it were not for the participation of horses. Come carnival time, wherever it may be, the horses of the area will always be seen, gaily decorated and wearing traditional harness, taking part in the processions and proceedings.

This elegant duo (plus lady friend riding side-saddle) were photographed in Seville, Spain and both horse and rider are wearing historic costume. Nearly all countries of the world have similar occasions—in the Camargue in France for example, there is an annual festival during which the famous black bulls of the area are rounded up by the cowboys or *gardiens* of the area mounted on the local Camargue ponies. The round-up is accompanied by further festivities in which the horses take part. In the Camargue region, there are many fêtes and carnivals which rely on the Camargue horses to bestow the atmosphere and pageantry that is associated with centuries of tradition. Local Camargue weddings too, nearly always feature the white horses to carry the bride and groom from the church.

47

SPORTING TYPES

When it comes to the sporting pursuits of the equestrian world, it seems certain that the horse enjoys his role every bit as much as the rider or driver urging him forward. Watch a racehorse as he waits tense and alert at the start of a race, every muscle braced for the starting signal; or the keen little polo ponies racing down the field after the ball, needing no signal from their rider to tell them when to wheel and turn. The noble carriage of the splendid horses that form a team of four pulling a coach on a marathon drive, or the jaunty step and proud demeanour of a Hackney pony striding out round a show ring are signs that the animal is happy in its work! And horses in the hunting field appear to have the 'thrill of the chase' infused in their blood, so keen and anxious are they not to be left behind.

Nearly all these sporting pursuits are as old as man's association with the horse. The first recorded mounted races date from a time well before the birth of Christ but they surely have a much longer unwritten history. After all, what easier way is there for man to show the supremacy of his horse over his neighbour's than if he can beat it in a race? Polo is an ancient game too and it is not hard to see why. It combines excitement, skill and speed with a team spirit that has always appealed to man. The various driving sports are probably a legacy from the great coaching days, although of course the art of driving horses dates from long before this time.

Hunting could well be the oldest sporting pursuit of all although it sprang from necessity—from the need to hunt and kill wild beasts for food. The most popular form of hunting today is fox-hunting although this only became popular towards the end of the 17th century. Before that it was the stag that was the most sought-after quarry.

STEEPLECHASING AND HURDLING

Previous page: Horse racing over a course of fences consists of two categories—steeplechasing and hurdling. In steeplechasing, the most popular and widely practised of the two, the jumps are constructed of thickly packed hard brush material, making fences that are both solid and imposing. Hurdle fences are made of soft brush and are considerably more flimsy. A horse brushing through them is unlikely to hurt himself while a similar action over a steeplechase fence would probably make a horse fall.

Steeplechasing began in the 1750s, a far cry from the organized, lucrative, crowd-drawing sport of today. In its very early days, it was no more than one country gentleman challenging another to a race across country to establish whose horse was the best. These races took a line from the steeple of one church to that of another—hence the name of steeplechasing. Now, the most famous steeplechase race of all—the Grand National—is held in the spring each year at the Aintree racecourse near Liverpool.

FLAT RACING

Above: The first record of a mounted horse race over a flat, measured distance is in 624BC at the thirty-third Olympiad held in ancient Greece. Since then the sport of flat racing has had a more chequered career than any other and has alternatively been known as the 'Sport of Kings' and the 'Pastime of the Devil'. Now a highly organized, international sport it attracts a huge following and involves some of the largest sums, both in prize money and wager stakes, of any equestrian sport.

The Thoroughbred horse is synonomous with the sport of racing and indeed is sometimes called the English Racehorse. This beautiful, lightly-built horse with its exquisite head and finely chiselled legs was produced by selective breeding, using three Arabian stallions as the foundation stock in the 18th century. It was first recorded as a breed in the General Stud Book in 1793 and was very much bred for speed rather than stamina. For this reason races on the flat are never over long distances.

THE FASTEST TEAM GAME

Above right: Not long after the date of the first flat race comes an equally authentic record of a game similar to polo being played. The game appears to have originated in Persia. It spread both east and west, although it was several centuries before this—the fastest of all team games in the world—reached the western world. It came to Britain with the army officers who had served in India and who, after seeing the game being played there, began to take part themselves. The first polo game to be played in England took place in the late 1860s and some 12 to 15 years later it had reached the USA too.

As with all sports, the rules and methods of play change slightly with successive generations, but as it is polo played today does not differ greatly from the game played by the British officers in India over a hundred years ago. It was played on the local manipuri ponies and was called *kangjai*. Silchar, the capital of the district of Cachar was the birthplace of modern polo with the oldest club in the world founded in 1859. Its members drew up the rules which form the basis of today's rules. When it was first played in London in 1869, people called it 'Hockey on horseback'. Two teams of four players compete, and because the game is played consistently at a gallop with fast turns and instantaneous stops which make it extremely tiring, it is divided into periods of play known as 'chukkas'. Riders change onto new mounts after each chukka, which lasts seven and a half or eight minutes. There may be anything from four to eight chukkas and as no pony can take part in more than three at the most in one day, polo players always have to have more than one pony in any one match.

Although there is no specific breed of horse or pony known as a polo pony, a very definite type is now recognized. The horse must be fast-moving but able to turn almost in its own length at high speeds. It must be able to come to a dead halt from a fast gallop and move off again just as quickly. Although always known as polo 'ponies', the allowed height is actually 15.3 hands high. Today the best polo ponies in the world come from Argentina.

51

THE TROTTING SPEEDSTERS

Right: Harness racing has its origins in the chariot races of Greek and Roman days and although, it is perhaps not as universally popular as flat racing and steeplechasing, it has not been subjected to as much criticism. Today, harness racing is divided into two distinct sporting categories—trotting and pacing. In the former, the horses trot at an extended version of the ordinary trot, diagonal pairs of legs (that is the hind leg on one side and the foreleg on the other) moving in unison. Pacers on the other hand, move the front and hind legs on one side of the body together. Although this is not a natural action for a horse, it has become so inbred into pacers that the young animals do it automatically.

In both trotting and pacing, the horses pound round a track pulling a light cart or 'sulky' in which the driving 'jockey' is seated. The horses must not change the pace; should they break into a canter they must be restrained back to a trot, which loses them valuable time.

Many countries of the world include trotting and pacing races in their sporting calendar—among them the United States of America, Canada, Russia and many European countries. Most countries where the sport is widely practised produce a special breed of trotter or pacer, the most famous being America's Standardbred. Like its flat-racing colleague the Thoroughbred, it is bred all over the world and includes both trotters and pacers. The name originated from the speed tests given to the early harness horses in which they had to cover a measured distance of ground in a standard time. The Standardbred usually stands about 15.2 hands high and has extremely powerful shoulders and hindquarters.

COACHING REVIVED

Below left and right: These impressive turn-outs of coaches drawn by four horses are a legacy from the great coaching era when the only way to travel long-distance was by stage coach (so called because they went from 'stage' to 'stage'). Ever since the coaching era began to wane as a result of motorization, there have been sportsmen reluctant to let the art of coaching die. The Coaching Club formed in 1871 has done much to keep this great sport alive and today it is enjoying a revival in many countries—particularly since HRH Prince Philip began to take an active interest in coach driving.

The Coaching Club requires its members to be able to drive a four-in-hand such as those illustrated here. The front two horses are known as leaders and the rear two are wheelers. The wheelers are responsible for slowing down the coach and act as brakes, while the leaders provide the main pulling power. The coaches are similar in design to the stage, mail and road coaches of the mid 19th century.

Official competitions are widely held for these sporting teams and come under the official jurisdiction of the international organisation that governs equestrian sport—the Fédération Equestre Internationale. The teams have to negotiate a cross-country course, where they must drive over rough ground, up and down hills and through water as well as an obstacle course when they have to drive forward and reverse through narrow spaces, step over poles and so on. In addition they have to complete a dressage test and will also be judged on their presentation and turn-out.

THE HIGH STEPPING HACKNEY

Above: Competition driving like this in which one horse or pony pulls a light trap or gig is also extremely popular. The horses and ponies most frequently used are a breed known as Hackneys which are renowned for their high-stepping gait.

The Hackney pony, such as the one seen here, is merely a small edition of the Hackney horse, descended from an extinct breed known as the Norfolk Trotter, later called the Norfolk Roadster. It was a short-legged, fast-trotting horse much used by those people who needed a reliable harness horse to help them in their daily work. The Roadster was made redundant by the railways but was revived later by the Hackney Breed Society. The Hackney horse's, most notable feature is its spectacular trotting action. The free shoulder movement allows the knee to be lifted high and the foreleg to be thrown well forward. Up to the beginning of this century, both Hackney horses and ponies were chiefly used by tradesmen to pull their carts as they went about their daily rounds. Now they are mainly seen in the show ring in smart turn-outs like this one and are very popular with the crowds.

A HANDSOME PAIR

Centre right: This is another smart private turn-out ('private' merely meaning that it is in private ownership rather than belonging to a firm or company and used for commercial purposes). Driving is by no means a cheap sport to pursue—harness and equipment are expensive items to purchase, not to mention the horses' upkeep. However, being less widely practised than it once was means that it is possible to buy second-hand vehicles. Providing they are in good repair, this can help to cut corners a little.

THE SCURRIERS

Right: This is one of the 'fun' driving competitions where the driver is often no older than the back-seat passenger in this picture. Known as pony scurry driving it involves piloting the keen little team round a complicated, winding course mapped out with plastic cones by the organisers. These cones are placed so that they are only fractionally wider than the four-wheeled dog carts, making it a race of accuracy and judgement. At some point during the competition, the driver has to halt the team and back the cart and ponies through a narrow space before taking off again. Scurry-driving competitions are held at major shows (this one was at Cardiff) and are a great favourite with the crowd. It is clearly fun for the 'coachman' and passenger—witness the expressions in the photograph—and the little ponies seem to enter into the spirit of the game. The ponies are seldom more than about 12.2 hands high and Shetland ponies—renowned for their prowess as harness ponies—are often seen competing in this event.

54

THE THRILL OF THE CHASE

Above left and right: Hunting is not a competitive sport, but it is undoubtedly a sporting pursuit. The term hunting today covers the pursuit of the fox, deer or hare with a pack of hounds. Of these it is fox-hunting that is the most widely followed. Hunting, of course, is no new phenomena—man has used horse and hound to pursue wild beasts for centuries. Originally it was to provide food for himself and his family, but for many hundreds of years it has been every bit as much a sporting hobby.

Packs of fox hounds belong to a 'hunt' and today there are about 200 hunts in existence in England and Wales. Each one has a clearly defined area and adjacent to its boundaries lies the country of another hunt. Unless hounds are in full cry after a fox, one hunt never encroaches upon the territory of another. Each hunt has a Master (in these days of high costs, this position is often held by two or more joint-masters) who is responsible for running the hunt, and a huntsman (who may also be the Master) whose job it is to actually hunt the hounds. He will be assisted by one or two Whipper-Ins who help him control hounds. The mounted followers are known as the Field, and they are usually organized and instructed by a Field Master.

Today many horsemen and women prefer a more humane way of enjoying the sport. This is drag-hunting, in which hounds, such as those above, follow a pre-determined line, laid by someone trailing the ground with a strong-smelling

substance such as aniseed. Hounds follow this scent, the field is assured a good day's ride and no blood is spilt.

The hounds used for hunting are specially trained for the work. They must be active and have a well-developed sense of smell. Beagles, bassets, bloodhounds, otterhounds, harriers and foxhounds are all suitable.

Hunting has become a very expensive sport. Subscriptions in Britain can be more than £100 for a season.

THE ROTHMAN TRADE TURN-OUT

Left: This smart coach-and-pair is known as a 'trade turn-out' for it belongs to a company, whose name it clearly carries. Rothmans of Pall Mall have owned it for many years and they use if for three main purposes. Every day, the coach and pair go from their mews stables and coach house in Knightsbridge to the company's office in Pall Mall, where they pick up deliveries to take to clubs, hotels and restaurants in London's West Eng. Its second use is for general promotional work. For example, it may go along to the opening of a new store where the company's products are to be sold. Its third job is that shown in this picture—to compete in trade shows and it makes about fifteen appearances in this capacity each year. The horses, called Pell and Mell, are both ex-Irish hunters. They are looked after by the two coachmen in this picture who are responsible for their well-being in addition to the smart turn-out of both them and the coach.

PICTURE GALLERY

Since prehistoric times, horses have repeatedly inspired man the artist. Prehistoric man expressed himself visually by drawing and painting on the walls of the caves in which he lived, thereby leaving valuable records for us, his descendants. One of the main subjects of such paintings, found in many parts of the world, is the horse. Since then artists from every generation—from Rembrandt to Renoir, Ucello to Leonardo da Vinci—have depicted horses in their paintings. Some of course painted horses merely as part of a general scene, because it would have been almost impossible to paint a scene of everyday life or a battleground that did not include horses. Others painted them to give added nobility and dignity to a portrait of a great man. In many of these, the horses are absurdly out of proportion in many details—not

least to their rider, from whose noble figure they were designed not to detract in any way. Some artists have painted the horse in its own right. Among the famous names are such people as Leonardo da Vinci with his anatomically detailed drawings of the horse, and the 18th century English painter George Stubbs, whose lifelike equestrian paintings are among the greatest the world has ever known. Stubbs was one of the few painters, who like da Vinci, made a proper study of his subject, thus producing a realistic image of the horse and not as the artist often used it, to complement the rest of the picture or the human subject.

Over the centuries horses have inspired not only great painters. Artists and craftsmen of every type,—sculptors, engravers, poets—have all repeatedly focused their skills upon horses. Athene's temple, and the Parthenon in Athens, dating from 438 BC, has some magnificent bas relief of horses, and even earlier examples of similar stone carving have been found. In almost every major town and city in the world there are statues of men on horseback—from Charlemagne at Aix-la-Chapelle to the Duke of Wellington who stands outside the Bank of England. The Chinese have some wonderful examples of early equestrian art in their superb porcelain figures, whilst bronze figures of horses and men have been discovered from Roman times and before.

INTO BATTLE

Previous page: The battleground has always fascinated artists and most famous battles have been committed to canvas by those anxious to record the details for posterity. The Battle of Waterloo, the Charge of the Light Brigade and the Battle of Omdurman have all been painted, some by numbers of artists. This aquatint by J. Harris after H. Martens depicts the charge of the 16th (Queen's Own) Lancers at Aliwal (145 kilometres: 90 miles south-east of Lahore) on the 28 January 1846. It was the third battle of the Seikh war in which 12,000 British and Indian troops, led by Sir Harry Smith, faced 20,000 Seikh troops under their leader, Runjur Singh. The Seikhs lost the battle, having been driven back across the River Sutlej. Three thousand of their men were reported dead or missing.

A NOBLE PORTRAIT

Above: Many soldiers and army officers have had their portraits painted whilst mounted on their favourite horse. This oil painting is of Cornet T. B. Parkyns, who served with the King's Light Dragoons (later to become the 15th Hussars) during the latter part of the eighteenth century. A Cornet, incidentally, is an officer in a troop of cavalry who carried the colours. Note how the artist here has painted the horse with incorrect proportions, in particular the tiny head which is perched at the end of a very long neck.

60

THE IMPRESSIONIST HORSES

Above: This jaunty little horse was painted by the French impressionist painter Henri Rousseau and is called *La Carriole du pere Juniet*. It hangs in the superb permanent exhibition of Impressionist paintings, housed in the Jeu de Paume, by the Tuileries Gardens in Paris.

Although horses were not a popular subject with the Impressionists, several of the great names of this artistic movement found a place for them in their works of art. Renoir was among them with a charming portrayal of an elegant side-saddle lady and her young charge entitled *Riding in the Bois de Boulogne*. Toulouse Lautrec and Edgar Degas, better known perhaps for their poignant circus figures and little ballerinas respectively, both made some wonderful studies of horses in the circus ring and on the race track.

CLASSICAL EQUITATION ON CANVAS

Left: The movements associated with haute école or classical equitation have captured the imagination of many artists over the centuries. This immaculate study is by Baron Reis d'Eisenberg.

Baron Reis d'Eisenberg created many more paintings of the airs on and above the ground which were modelled at the Spanish Riding School of Vienna. They may now be seen at Wilton House in Salisbury, England.

HORSES IMMORTALIZED IN STONE

The statues and fountains illustrated on these two pages are at Chantilly in the Ile de France (*above and far left*) and Salzburg, in Austria (*left*). Both of these places have a long established association with and considerable reverence for the horse.

Chantilly's association stems from its famous chateau where the stabling for 420 horses is still used today. Built in the 18th century by the Duc de Condé the stables provided accommodation for the horses and the 420 hounds, kept for stag hunting.

In Salzburg, there are many examples of this city's long-held respect for the noble animal. Torrents of water stream from the nostrils of a number of horses on this statue situated in Kapitelplatz where there is also a small watering trough, put there originally for the convenience of the 'horses of the church dignitaries'. Not far away, in Sigmunds-platz, there is a large watering trough designed especially for the archbishop's horses. Around it there is a series of frescoes depicting prancing horses and the Platz also contains a statue dedicated to the horse.

The horses sculpted out of stone over a church doorway (*above*) provide an excellent example of how artists do not always get everything quite right. If a horse had as many teeth, it would be unable to shut its mouth! Many sculptors, more concerned with the human element of the compositions have failed to study their horse 'model' in sufficient detail.

If you look at some statues carefully, you may very well find a number of errors—from the number of teeth, to the proportion of the horse's head to its body, to its improbable stance.

PONIES AT PLAY

Riding for pleasure and fun has become the major role of the horse over the last 30 or 40 years. Before that time far more people owned horses because they wanted to put them to work than because they found riding a relaxing hobby and a pleasant way to pass the weekend. Only a comparatively few people, mainly of the moneyed classes or aristocracy, owned horses and ponies for recreational purposes and they certainly did not have the fun with them that most people enjoy today.

It is the dream of every child—and many an adult—who becomes bitten with the 'horsey bug' to have their own horse or pony. For many it remains only a dream but this does not bar the way to being able to ride or even to learning how to look after and care for a pony. Riding is equally no longer some-

thing only for wealthy people—instead it has come within the reach of just about everybody, provided they are keen enough to find ways of overcoming any obstacles or difficulties that might stand in the way. Most people learn to ride at riding schools and a great number of such establishments are willing for pupils to help with the stable chores at the school in return for the occasional ride.

It is not only country dwellers who are able to own a horse or pony; more and more people who live in towns and cities have found a way to overcome the lack of grazing or land for stabling—by keeping their horse at livery. Even in major cities there are numbers of livery stables; where people can keep their horses.

If you are lucky enough to have a horse or pony bought for you, do make sure first that you have both the knowledge and the facilities to care for it properly. Seek expert help and advice when looking for a pony to buy and take the advice given. It is easy to fall in love with a pony that might, for any number of reasons, be quite unsuitable for you, and that may then prove to be difficult to sell to someone else.

One of the great leisure areas in riding nowadays is in pony trekking and riding holidays. To go on a casual pony trekking holiday, in most cases, needs no expert riding ability and indeed, many people have had their introduction to the joys of horseback by going on a trekking holiday.

GYMKHANA GAMES

Gymkhana games are a favourite with all children who enjoy riding and it is an area of competition in which the winning ponies are by no means always the best bred or the most expensive. Providing a young rider is prepared to devote time, energy and patience to careful training and constant practice, almost any pony can be taught the rudiments of gymkhana games and most seem to thoroughly enjoy the friendly knockabout competitions.

There are many classic gymkhana games and every year, organizers of the events all over the country dream up new ideas to test the skill of pony and rider. On the opposite page, two of the classic games are underway. At the top a bending race is in progress; in this event several lines of poles are placed in the ground in straight lines. The riders race up and down them, weaving in and out of the poles; the first one back to the starting line being the winner. Below this, riders are taking part in a sack race. In this they race up to a given line holding a sack; then they must jump off their ponies, climb into the sack and hop back to the starting line, leading their ponies behind them. Above, two young riders race against one another to test their pony's speed, while to the left a young rider is putting her all into urging her pony forward!

The successful gymkhana pony will be one that is nimble, agile and speedy, able to get off to a flying start and stop just as quickly when required. It must also not be perturbed by unusual objects or noises, such as balloons popping in its face, for these are all part of gymkhana games.

A gymkhana is usually the young riders introduction to the world of showjumping and competitive events. Nearly all the famous showjumping stars of today began on their road to success by entering their local gymkhanas.

JUNIOR CROSS-COUNTRY

Previous page: Biting her lip in concentration, a young rider clears a post and rails fence with room to spare. Although in this case the jump is part of a competition course, it provides a good example of how easy it is to build your own practice fences. The poles are supported at either end by a wooden pole, but for a practice jump the poles could be wedged into a couple of solid, conveniently-placed bushes like these. The pole on the ground forms a 'ground line' making it easier for rider and pony to judge the take-off point.

WINTER WARMTH

Above: A close look at this woolly little pony grazing in the New Forest, in Hampshire, will show how such ponies are able to live out-of-doors and survive the harshest winters. That thick fluffy coat is not just a winter overcoat to keep out the cold; the natural grease it contains also makes it waterproof so that it keeps out the rain. If you have ever looked at a small, scruffy pony in a heavy rain storm, you will notice how the rain runs over the coat in little rivers and drips away. Ponies kept at grass should not be given any thorough grooming in the wintertime as brushing removes the grease from the coat. Once this has gone, they have no natural protection against wet conditions and they will soon catch cold. The only grooming necessary for a pony at grass in the winter is to remove dried mud from the legs and coat, free the mane and tail from tangles and clean out the feet.

HOLIDAYS WITH HORSES

Centre right: Keeping horses and ponies is very often a family affair, which means that the responsibility and time needed can be shared. Or if a family does not own their own horse or pony, they might want to go on a 'horsey holiday' together as this French family have done. Holidays involving horses need not necessarily mean taking to the saddle and actually riding, although trekking holidays are probably the most popular equestrian vacation. Instead you can do as the young member of this family is doing and learn how to be the jockey behind a trotting horse. Courses in nearly all aspects of horsemanship are available—from riding side-saddle to learning the rudiments of stud management and how to look after a mare and newly born foal.

THE FARRIER AT WORK

Opposite: All horses and ponies that are ridden or put to work in any way must have their feet shod with iron shoes. This is because hard roads and stony tracks soon wear down the animal's hooves and expose the sensitive areas of the foot. If this were to happen, in no time at all the pony would go lame and be unfit to ride. Regularly every month or six weeks, the farrier should take off the shoes and trim the feet.

Shoeing is done in one of two ways—by the hot or cold method. In hot shoeing, the farrier heats the shoes in the furnace until they are red hot; then he places each one against the horse's hooves. In spite of the smoke and even flames that occur as the dead horn burns away, the horse feels nothing, which is apparent from the way he does not flinch. In the cold method, the shoe is not heated, instead it is both fitted and hammered on to the hoof whilst completely cold.

SHOW HORSES

The show horse—be it a hack or hunter, a show pony or a mountain or moorland mare with her foal at her side—is the most beautiful of all horses, for such is its reason for existing. A show horse is one that is of sufficient good looks and conformation, combined with good paces and manners, to compete against others of similar characteristics in the show ring. It is undoubtedly in the show ring that one will see the finest examples of horse-flesh, at least in appearance, and to the non-expert, each one looks every bit as beautiful as the one standing next to it.

Horse shows are now dominated by the exciting

jumping classes, but in fact they first came into being as show-places for horses. They provided the opportunity for the breeders to show the world what they had been able to produce, and the inevitable spirit of competition generally led to the improvement of the breed. Many shows today are still held just for a specific breed or type. There is an Arabian horse show, for example, comprising only of classes for different categories of Arabian horse. The Palomino Society has its own show in which only Palomino horses and ponies can compete.

Show horses and ponies command fantastic prices when they change hands and yet their life is really confined to the show ring. One little blemish to a show hack or pony means it can no longer expect to be among the top ranks of the rosette winners, so few owners of such an animal are prepared to run the risk of allowing it to receive such injury. This means a show hunter is seldom seen in the hunting field, nor does a show pony compete in the 'rough and tumble' games of a local gymkhana.

There is a place in the show ring for the rather more 'commonplace' horses and ponies, however, in what are termed the 'working' classes. In working hunter and pony classes, entrants have to jump a small jump and may be asked to do several other things, such as opening a gate, or reversing through two closely-positioned hurdles. They are judged more on performance than appearance and the inclusion of such events at many shows has helped to open up the show world to a great number of would-be competitiors.

CHAMPION HUNTER

Previous page: The rosette on this show hunter's bridle and the smile on his rider's face indicate that he has just been awarded the champion position at the show. Although he has won his class as a 'hunter' it is unlikely that this horse has ever been near the hunting field! Classes for show hunters are divided into a number of categories—lightweight, middleweight and heavyweight are the usual divisions but larger shows may also have classes for working hunters, ladies' hunters and four-year-olds.

THE JUDGE'S DECISION IS FINAL!

Left: Unlike show jumping or gymkhana games where the winner of the competition depends entirely on who performs the best according to the rules that govern the event, in the world of showing, the results often depend to a large extent on the judge's individual preferences. Judges, of course, follow the accepted standards laid down for the type of horse they are judging, but their particular likes and dislikes must also play a part. Here lady judges are assessing the conformation of a hack and later they will also ride it. Like a hunter, a hack is a type of horse rather than a breed. Very much a ladies' horse, it is a lightweight animal of exceptional elegant appearance, with beautiful smooth paces and perfect manners. The last two points are ones the judges will be looking for particularly when they ride each horse.

The name hack is derived from the word *haquerai* used in the Middle Ages for horses of humble origin. Although it now strictly applies to any horse on which one goes for a 'hack'—that is a ride, it is more usually used to describe these show horses.

CONNEMARA MARE AND FOAL

Above: Showing classes are by no means always ridden—many, in which the horses or ponies are led are known as 'in-hand' classes. Such classes are usually for specific breeds and many breed societies have their own shows. Classes may be for brood mares, mares and foals, yearlings (horses or ponies that are between one and two years) and two-year-olds or they may be for the best of the breed whatever the age. Arabian horses (see page 12) are often shown in-hand. Here a Connemara mare and her foal are lined-up in front of the camera. The Connemara is one of Great Britain's mountain and moorland breeds. It is of ancient origin and comes from the Connaught Province of Ireland. Its pretty appearance owes something to the infusion of Arabian blood into the breed.

THE PERFECT PONY

Above: Many small and all major shows have a number of classes for show ponies. The show pony is not a breed—it is merely a pony of beautiful appearance, pretty paces and impeccable manners. Providing a pony possesses such attributes, it is perfectly entitled to be entered in a show. Classes for show ponies are usually divided into height limits—up to 12.2 hands high, up to 13.2 hands high and up to 14.2 hands high. Ponies that consistently win these classes at big shows are extremely valuable and might well change hands for £10,000 or more, which seems a great deal to pay for one small pony!

CARE AT THE SHOW

Right: How a rider looks after his pony at a show can tell you a lot about the way that person cares for the animal in general! People who take their ponies to shows, ride them round the ground endlessly all day in between classes, or tie them up in the sun with no bucket of water close by are certainly not giving their ponies the consideration they would want themselves. This pony is more fortunate; he has been tethered to the back of the horse box and given a full net of hay to occupy him. In addition, his thoughtful owner has attached a fly net to his head collar to keep the flies away from his eyes. Flies can be a constant irritation to horses and ponies, buzzing in to the corners of their eyes and around their faces. A field shelter is used more in the summer as a place to escape the flies than in winter as a protection against bad weather.

TUG-OF-WAR

Above: A young foal can be remarkably strong as this lad is finding to his cost! Such a situation is made worse by the fact that at this age, the foal has only been broken to a head-collar and has not yet had a bit in his mouth or a bridle on his head, so the person leading him has very little means of control. Like most young animals, foals are naturally frisky and such displays of high spirits are to be expected. Foals should be broken to wearing a head-collar at a young age; Thoroughbred foals, for example, generally have their first experience of a head-collar when they are only one or two days old and soon after that they will be taught to lead. Non-thoroughbred foals will probably have a considerably longer period of freedom before being disciplined.

PRACTICE MAKES PERFECT

Left: A young side-saddle rider puts her pretty show pony through its paces in a practice paddock at home. Not very many years ago, girls and ladies always rode side-saddle and none would consider such an unlady-like pursuit as riding astride! Now side-saddle riding is something of a dying art, which is a pity for there is nothing more elegant than an impeccably attired lady riding side-saddle on an equally well turned-out hack. This is an unusual sight of a side-saddle rider, for when dressed in the proper clothes, the skirt of the side-saddle habit completely covers her legs. Horses and ponies must be trained to carry a side-saddle rider—those broken in to an ordinary astride saddle do not always take kindly to having a side-saddle on their backs.

THE LONDON HARNESS HORSE PARADE

The London Harness Horse Parade is a show that has been held each year in Regent's Park since 1965, under the auspices of The London Harness Horse Parade Society. This society was formed by the amalgamation with the London Cart Horse Parade Society. An indication of the waning interest and use of heavy horses can be seen from the figures attached to the Parades of the London Cart Horse Society prior to amalgamation. Up to 1914 entries had to be restricted to 1000 but by 1965, there were only 26 entries. The London Van Horse Parade used to restrict those allowed to compete to light commercial horses and ponies, but under the new rulings heavy horse turn-outs as well as private driving vehicles are allowed to enter. Each entry is judged on turn-out and performance as it trots round the outer circle of Regent's Park.

The main aims of the Society in holding the parade are
—To improve the general condition, treatment and management of horses and ponies.
—To encourage those in charge of horses and ponies employed for transport purposes to take a humane and intelligent interest in their well-being and to show a spirit of kindliness towards their animals.
—To encourage and assist all those using horse-drawn transport to achieve a high standard of care and cleanliness.

The basic parts of the driving harness are the bridle, the collar with traces, the pad or saddle which support the shafts or traces, and the breeching.

Above is a smart little Welsh cob drawing a well-laden cart. To the right is a rather more sombre turn-out pictured at a similar event.

INDEX

ACKNOWLEDGMENTS

The author and publishers would like to thank the following persons and organisations for their help in producing this book: Cinematie, Paris: 60 bottom, 61 bottom; French Government Tourist Office: 68 centre; Leslie Lane: 40-1 top; National Army Museum: 58-9, 60 top; Peter Roberts: 2-3, 6-7, 8-9, 15, 16-17, 18, 19, 20, 21, 22, 23, 26, 27, 28, 29, 30 centre & bottom, 32 bottom, 33, 34-5, 36-7, 40 bottom, 41 bottom, 44 top, 52 bottom left & right, 54, 55, 56 bottom, 62, 63, 66, 67, 69, 70-1, 72, 73, 74, 75, 76, 77; Sally Anne Thompson: 10-11, 12 top & bottom left, 13, 14, 24-5, 30 top 31 top, 42 left, 42-3 top, 64-5, 68 top; Tourist Office, Zermatt: 32 top; US Travel Service: 12 bottom right, 44 centre, 45; Zefa: 38, 39, 46, 47, 48-9, 50, 51, 52-3 top, 56 top, 57.

PDO 79-399